D0870219

ADVANCE PRAISE FOR *THE PATH OF LONELINESS*:

"Yet again, Candice James has produced a beautiful and heartwarming collection of poetry. A lovely set of poems on landscape, love, and loneliness that gently unfold to leave the reader moved, transported and inspired. Each line is a soaring melody and when the lines are combined into a powerful whole you have your very own complete symphony."
—**ALAN HILL,** Poet Laureate, New Westminster, BC, and author of *We Came from Water* and *Narrow Road to the Far West*

"Candice James is a poet of versatility and expansion. In this collection, *The Path of Loneliness,* she takes the reader on a journey of the heart. My favourite poem, "Again and Again," speaks of the infinite and the ordinary, in a way that uses cadence to reinforce the impossible. Candice's own strong musical background is the golden thread these poems are attached to. Beautiful language and sparkling imagery make *The Path of Loneliness* relevant and vital."
—**JUDE NEALE,** author of *Impromptu* and *Splendid in its Silence*

"Of loneliness much has been said. More reflections emerge as we navigate the isolating, unembracing times of COVID-19. But here, Candice James paints the purple of being lonely in love. With another brush, the dusty lonely of loss. With another, the shadows of colonized star. All this, on an empty canvas of loneliness as a choice to be made and remade."
—**SALIMAH VALIANI,** author of *Land of the Sky* and *Cradles*

"In these poems, Candice James confronts a world of disappointment, loss and sadness when the scintillating promise of romantic love dies. In *The Path of*

Loneliness the journey is one marked by the ghosts of past loves, of regret and unspoken, un-lived intentions. Yet, the way travelled is one of persistence of the soul and spirit to rise through all the elements: air, fire, water, dust to come through. The poet's destination is a place of art, music and most of all, poetry. In the poem "Poets' Dance," James invites us in, "... where liquid, quicksilver lightning / shakes the foundations of the mind / and rocks the questing heart...." Poems of sorrow and dashed hope arrive at the joyful conclusion in the beautifully rhymed final poem: "...something still breathes ... alive in the paint."

—**PAM GALLOWAY,** author of *Passing Stranger* and *Parallel Lines*

The Path of
Loneliness

The publisher gratefully acknowledges the support of the Canada Council for the Arts and the Ontario Arts Council. The publisher is also grateful for the financial assistance received from the Government of Canada.

Front cover artwork: Candice James, "The Path of Loneliness," 2016, acrylic on canvas, 20 x 16 inches.

Cover design: Val Fullard

Library and Archives Canada Cataloguing in Publication

Title: The path of loneliness : poems / Candice James.
Names: James, Candice, 1948- author.
Series: Inanna poetry & fiction series.
Description: Series statement: Inanna poetry & fiction series
Identifiers: Canadiana (print) 20200208284 | Canadiana (ebook) 20200208306 |
ISBN 9781771337618 (softcover) | ISBN 9781771337625 (epub) |
ISBN 9781771337632 (Kindle) | ISBN 9781771337649 (pdf)
Classification: LCC PS8569.A429 P38 2020 | DDC C811/.54—dc23

Printed and bound in Canada

Inanna Publications and Education Inc.
210 Founders College, York University
4700 Keele Street, Toronto, Ontario M3J 1P3 Canada
Telephone: (416) 736–5356   Fax (416) 736–5765
Email: inanna.publications@inanna.ca Website: www.inanna.ca

The Path of Loneliness

POEMS BY

Candice James

Inanna Poetry & Fiction Series

INANNA Publications & Education Inc.
Toronto, Canada

ALSO BY CANDICE JAMES

A Split in the Water (1979)
Inner Heart, A Journey (2010)
Bridges and Clouds (2011)
Midnight Embers – A Book of Sonnets (2012)
Shorelines – A Book of Villanelles (2013)
Ekphrasticism – Painted Words (2013)
Purple Haze (2014)
A Silence of Echoes (2014)
Merging Dimensions (2015)
Short Shots (2016)
Colours of India (2016)
City of Dreams (2017)
The Water Poems (2017)
The 13th Cusp (2018)
Rithimus Aeternam (2019)

I thank those who have crossed my path and lingered awhile.
You have made the journey less lonely.

Contents

Faces of Love

Veil

Spirit

Surreal

I have more memories
than if I were a thousand years old.

—Charles Baudelaire

Degrees

Degrees of Depth

I wait

    while

        a lonely
        violin

        whispers
        softly
            through
            the shadows

You approach

    and suddenly

        the world
          is
        a symphony

Falling Reins

Two pairs of eyes,
           locked in the embrace
                      of each other's silent thoughts.

Holes being slowly, methodically bored
           inside each other's soul
                      to allow the intense build-up of heat to
                                          escape.

Our minds
           casually shutting down
               each and every safety valve
                    with a knowing precision.

                      Proximity melting
           to singularity
                    and plurality
                            simultaneously.

And what of these bodies?
      Shall we release the reins
or grip them tighter yet?

Two people
        making love to each other
    in their thoughts;
    spinning them real.

The only sound they hear:

            the faint whisper
                of the falling reins.

Feelings and Flesh

I fall through
> your desperate dreams
> like a shooting star

lost in feelings
> and flesh
> inside the blanket of night.

You draw me in easily
> onto the steep black cliffs

> > of your heart
> and   e-x-p-a-n-d   the lakes
> in   my   eyes.

A misty spirit,

> I huddle
> in the damp aftermath;

A desperado,

> forever free-falling
> through your desperate dreams,

> lost

> in your tantric maze
> of feelings and flesh.

Language and Landscapes

There are recognized words
and foreign languages.
　　　There are well known horizons
　　　and alien landscapes…

　　　　　and then there is you
　　　　　　　sandwiched somewhere between.

I know you
in timbres of sound,
sensations of touch,
obscure visuals.

　　　The fluid whisper
　　　of your lips and fingers
　　　dance across my body;
　　　create the abstract painting
　　　I dwell in.

　　　　　You are my world.

　　　　　Language and landscapes
　　　　　are unrequired.

The Wind and I

In an obscure sign language,
    I etch words in the air,
        and scratch emotions onto
    the supple back of the wind,
        in a farscape of dust and stars.

Through the mist, approaching me,
waxing brighter as it nears me,
           I see your fabulous face.

The wind and I know who you are.
    We trade secrets and identities
        as we kiss your lips,
           tousle your hair
        and fight to stake our claims
  on your body and soul,
        carving our names indelibly
           into your blood and bone.

As we tighten our embrace,
    the dust and stars are crumbling,
        the farscape is dissolving,
           and the words I etched in the air,
           are indelibly engraved
             on our hearts.

Saviour Mine

You tried to tell me who you were.
    I did not listen,
        my hands over my ears.

You tried to show me that part of you I never saw.
    I did not look,
        closed my hands over my eyes
            as I walked away
                from your familiar touch
            and the face I once recognized
                as the best part of me;
                    the part of me
                        that now lay flayed out on a canvas
                so far behind me
            I could no longer see it.

            You were the artist
                but you did not come
                    to see me walk away in sorrow.

I turned around
            and looked at all I was leaving behind
        and I thought about you,
                with a sense of loss.

I turned to stone;
        a statue standing in harm's way.
I allowed myself to be crushed
        by the locomotive of emotion
thundering down the track
        toward my stiff inglorious body.

But I didn't die as I'd planned that day.

Much time, many years passed
    in a matter of seconds;
        in the blink of an eye.
            I was lost in a minor symphony of suspended tears
                that cost too much to produce.

Now I bargain for a ticket to anywhere.
    I offer songs for alms.
      I beg for mercy
        and long for your familiar touch.
                I pray to recluse angels for aid.
        Reluctantly their weary wings transition
    into delicate threads becoming
ropes of hope,

I climb out of myself,
        out of the cold, endless night
           and I'm blinded by the light at first sight.
        At second sight
            I see your shining face
        And I recognize myself

as the fallen;
and you as the one
sworn to a throne most high.

I swim inside your all-consuming eyes;
and finally recognize you
for who you truly are…
my Saviour.

Moon Shadows

Tonight the ocean dilates
       in the slick of the moon,
              spilling onto the shorelines we walk.

Our shadows,
       illuminated in shafts of silver light,
       follow us relentlessly, tirelessly
       trying to catch us to feel:
              The damp sand between our toes.
              The touch of our clasped hands.
              The whisper of our breath.
              The heat of our lips when we kiss.

Tomorrow, under a brilliant sun,
       we'll walk the streets of tall buildings
       beside our shadows cast on the walls:
              slowing our pace;
              leaning against them;
              melting into them
          for a short breath in time
        until the ocean dilates
       in the slick of the moon once again,
and our shadows chase us down.

As we walk this familiar shoreline
of moon shadows,
far flung from the streets of tall buildings
and tomorrow's brilliant sun,
we'll dance in moon shadows
until the darkness undresses.

Alone

Alone

Although you walk with me,
      I walk alone
           familiarizing myself with
                certain and uncertain brands of emptiness,

    travelling rocky trails,
        witnessing the journey
           through faded eyes
      and yesterday smiles.

        Born alone…
           we pass away alone.

        This is our journey.
           We all walk alone.

      You alone
        have made my journey
           less lonely.

The Path of Loneliness

I have chosen the path of loneliness
        yet there are many people near me and around me.
            They do not know I have chosen this path.
            They do not see me as I really am.

On this path,
        soul travelling alone,
            I have come upon many men:
                Spent time with some.
                    Spent love with others.

        And then…
            I came upon a man called music.

             I wrote songs,
                played melodies
            and made love with him
        for many years.

        And then…
        I left him,
            our music,
                and myself.

        I locked my guitar in its case
     so it could be silenced
and call to me no more.

I turned back to my roots,
to my poetry.

I travelled the breadth and depth of my soul
pulling out truisms,
wisdom and lies;

mixing them
into a potpourri of words and rhyme
trying to make sense of where I'd been;
hoping to find out where I was going;
searching for that part of me
that was already lost before I took my first breath.

I have no friends;
only acquaintances.
They haze in
and out
of my checkerboard house
never noticing the rooms are bare
and the faded paint is peeling
into surreal slices of wasted time and space;

and now, as the sky bends down to embrace me,
I am tangled in the vines of regret.

My eyes mist over with the realization
of the many wrongs I cannot right.

I have chosen this path of loneliness;
and all things considered,
given the chance,
I would choose it again.

Surreal Evening

Inside this surreal evening,
I walk alone
      whispering secrets to the wind,
      that echo softly
            across a pale, yellow sky.
Slices of shadow shimmer,
      and dust the fading aura
            of a weary city
            falling asleep.

A Surreal evening
      dissolving the sins of the day,
      dancing through the trees,
            kisses the breeze,
         bringing the world to its knees
     in silent prayer
    until all is forgiven,
            cleansed,
            chaste once again.

A Surreal evening
         spins on torn and tossed winds
     scattering stardust;
       dissolving
   in the misty tears
      of a dying sun

under the half-mast eyelids
of a pale yellow sky.

                    Both of us…
                    old beyond our years.

The Panther's Paw

I came from my own galaxy,
      riding on a diamond laser beam
            that sliced through the ocean
                as the sky flew away
                    singing a song from my past
                in tune and time to the turn
                    of the windmills in my mind.
I wept:
      One tear echoing home.
      The second tear crushing the unspoken questions
            perched on the cut glass precipice of my lips.

                  The pier and vagrant tugboats
                      swayed silently
                      where gulls didn't nest anymore.

                I wished upon a star
            falling from the panther's paw.

Circles, jagged and obtuse
      led to abstract answers
            dissolving in waves
                always too far away,
                    just beyond reach.
                      In my nightmares they scream and shout
                in languages I can't understand.
            They stir like a living spoon
through the mulch and mix of my imagination.

I touched a star
    falling from the panther's paw.

I've forgotten who I am,
    can't recall my true self.

I've altered my universe.
    Changed it,
  and,
    witnessing the moon
    voraciously lift the negligee of night,
I feel only slight shame at my voyeurism.

As my spirit sheds its skin in layers,
    I stand in naked awe
      and languish inside a glorious seven-year itch,
        whispering sweet nothings
          from underneath the stage of life
          until I lose my voice,
          my words,
          my sense of time and place;
        and totally forget who I really am,
or who I ever once was.

I become the falling star
    returning to the panther's paw.

I become
    night never-ending.

Almost

All the houses I've called home
                     have crumbled to dust.

The sidewalks I once walked
          are cracked and buckled now
                  under the pressure of herculean weeds,
                          the residue of festered seeds.

        Somewhere behind the dead hedge,
            beneath the bare branches of the age-old broom tree
          I played in, and on, as a child,
              there lives the still beating heart
              of a dream I could never lay to rest.

I can still glimpse little chunks of the other me
      I never allowed to be born,
         glistening and gleaming in tiny shards of stained glass mirrors,
                 hazing in   and out
             at the core of a rainbow city
             I never visited or lived in.

       I was almost two people
                 becoming four, six, eight, ten, eleven;
                 but really only one ...
                 becoming none.

All the houses I've ever called home

                            have crumbled to dust

     almost…
     like they never were;

                            almost…
                            like I never was.

Oblique

There is a location called mine,
known yet unknown to me,

        in this place I am;
        in this place I will never be.

I am a being
with no substance or essence,

        seen but obscure,
        flashing off and on,
        walking with millions
        yet walking alone always.

More here and less there.
More there and less here

        entwined in my karma,
        far from my destiny,
        all my letters arriving
        in sealed vacuums.

The horizon colours the sky
and colonizes the stars'
glorious surreal architecture;

        but in this location,
        known yet unknown to me,
        I am but will never be.

This is the place of oblique lenses,
distorted mirrors, closed doors left ajar

where it is not possible to enter or exit.

I am here but can never arrive.

So it is and will never be.
So I am and will ever be,
disposition dislocated;
an exercise in futility.

Again and Again

I am the birth of all things
        waiting to be born again,

                and reborn…

                    again and again.

I have lingered in tall grasses
on the hillsides, on the moors,
        and heard the haunting echoes
        of long vanished bagpipes.

        I have parted clouds to view a deeper sky.
I have listened with a fervent vengeance
        and heard the rush of angels mingling with me
                as if I were an intricate part of them.

                I have felt the pulse of their heartbeat
                    echoing softly against my chest
                    and been touched by droplets
                        of crimson blood and silver ink
                    whetting words of wisdom,
                perched on the angels' lips,
        spilling them onto the scrolls of life.

Bearing my cross for all to see
        I have carried my sins with me;
                and yet they remain invisible
                    to those eyes that will not see.

I have done these things

                with a pure soul
                but still have not graduated
                        into the purity of light.

        Again and again...
                I am the preparation not the meal.

        Again and again…
                I am the dampness not the rain.

I have flown wingless
        through layers of air
                leaving remnants of my flesh behind,
                        as scars to remember me by,
                                lest the universe forgets I passed this way.

        I have worshipped in churches
        with blood-stained windows.
                I have gazed through iron eyes
                and read from silver scrolls burnt black;
                        charred beyond recognition.

        I have become the laughter of saints
        and the sorrow of unblessed saviours.

                I am the death of all life
                waiting to be shaped again,

                    and reshaped…

                            again and again.

A Tricky Thing

The past is a tricky thing:
                        a cavalcade of images
                        sometimes dissolved in water;
                        sometimes etched in stone.

Viewed through rose-coloured glasses
                the hard-edged glare softens;
                        memories glisten beneath stardust.

In the hard light of day:
                        a wheel of emotions;
                        a see-saw of ups and downs;
                        sometimes smooth as satin;
                        sometimes rough as sandpaper.

The road is long and winding
from the past to the present
with many unscheduled stops:
                        some a dream come true;
                        some a stifling nightmare.

In the stone-cold sober aftermath of the tricky past,
        or at the bottom of the half-full glass of the shaky present;
                somewhere, at the quantum level,
        in our house of mirrors,
                in our own personal universe,

the present becomes obsessed with its own distorted past
and wonders…

how it ever got this way.

The past is a tricky thing.

It never really fades away.
It has a way of sneaking up on you
when you least expect it.
The past is…

a tricky thing.

Broken Wishing Well

Walking down a quarter line,
    half past yesterday
        and running out of time,
    there are flowers
            I long to stop and smell.

    So many wishes wasted;
    left lying there,
    dying there,
    in life's broken wishing well.

        So many good intentions,
        scattered pell-mell,
        stumbled and fell
        on the road to hell.

The ghosts of old lovers that hold a grudge
    loom large on my horizon:
        some in war-torn blue jeans,
    some with suits and ties on.

Drifting and dancing
through the streets and doorways
            of my tangled mind
            I see myself unwinding
        and scattering   pell-mell
          at the bottom
        of life's broken wishing well.

Out of Touch

I've been out of touch,
stirring the echoes in my mind,
sifting through mirrored jigsaw puzzle pieces of the past,
trying to put myself together again
with the cart behind the horse,
on earth as it isn't,
in the stir of echoes I swirl in.

These scattered pieces of mirror
gleaming in shallow pools of blood,
shed from old wounds never laid to rest,
lay beside a shiny new shovel
with my name emblazoned on it.

Suddenly I turn to metal.
The shovel jumps over the moon,
lands in my hands
and begs me to dig.

I unearth the horse and cart
I've been searching for;
rearrange them, cart before the horse.

The stir of echoes slows, then stills.
I clasp my left hand with my right,
Back in touch with myself.

Movement

I move through this world alone in a crowd;

                                  alone ... but not lonely.

I move through this world
            laughing, with companions,
                dining with friends,
                     spending time with acquaintances.

       I seem present
                 but still, I remain apart ... and alone.

I move through this world on two different paths:
                        one of the world,
                        public domain.
             One of my own,
             private ruminations.

       Remembering the past,
            living with people:
            dead people that once drew breath and lived
                   the good life, the high life,
                     the night life ... *my life.*
            dead people that truly mattered
                 and still matter.

I move through this world
            with my ghosts close,
                 drawing nearer every day.

A Lonely Guitar Breeze

A lonely guitar breeze strums
the memories of my mind

        and everywhere
          I look I find

                short flashes of white,
                  a fading twilight;

                    but no respite,
                    no saving grace
                    to light the nights.

      I'm an outlaw riding
    with an old dusty heartache
      and the dull fading glint
      of an old rusty keepsake.

                    There's emptiness
                  filled with damp whispers
            swaying inside the cradle of night

        and a lonely guitar breeze
           stirring old memories;

                    some better left alone.

Faces of Love

Even Now

Saturday, early evening, December;
      neon moon glinting buffed beams
            polishing icy blue diamonds
            to a fine glitter and shine
            on the snow glazed street below.

We sat in creamy contentment,
sunken into the lush velvet sofa,
listening to the soft, satin voicings of Sinatra
and the echo of our heartbeats
as the snowflakes drifted and fell...
drifted, drifted and fell.

      On that cold December night
      in a summer state of mind
            I looked into your eyes
      and saw the promise
      of another sunburnt July
            drying wanton teardrops
               falling from the sky's eye.

Then came January evenings.
strong moons and ice glazed stars
dripping sequined teardrops
onto the broken dance floor
we circled so casually;
oblivious to the sharp edges
and destruction that lay ahead.

Years later,
alone on a sailboat
off the southern edge
of the Florida Keys.

I keep running the film:
Backward and forward.
Forward and backward.

What I did and didn't do.
What you did and didn't say.

Not knowing then, or even now,
what you were thinking.

On the deck in the cabin
there is a photo of us standing,
glinting beneath a neon moon
and a stack of love letters I wrote
but never did send to you.

Earlier today I wrote another letter to you:
pouring my heart out,
crying my eyes out,
kissing the tear-stained pages,
knowing I'd never send them to you.

I reach for my guitar in the corner
and I become the gypsy singer

you fell in love with long, long ago
on a cold December night.

        I imagine you, tonight, high up on a mountain,
    on the other side of the world where snow is softly falling
        and wonder if you're remembering too.

            I want to tell you everything;

                        even now,
                        after all this time,

                            I can't.

Lost Edge

I've lost my edge
    in synch with the fading essence of my perfume.
        I am half-sleeping beside the television,
one eye peeled, watching all the stations at once.
           In the corner of my mind a jukebox starts to play.
             The strings on my guitar begin to hum
                under the strum and ghostly caress
          of a lost wayfarer, invisible in this realm.

    There is a hollowed out static
    in this rolling ocean of subtle sound.

I wait for the silence between beats,
    which I know must inevitably come,
        to stretch the deafening noise
           into a band of endless echoes.

I wait and wait.
      I am half-asleep
           wrapped in this limitless void.

The telephone rings.
        I answer it with a frenzied urgency,
                grasping for straw dogs on broken leashes,
       held in check by ragged scarecrows;
hoping to hear your voice once again,
                     if only to hear you say "It's over."

But it's not you;

        and I've lost my edge
            in synch with the fading essence
     of my perfume and …
            you're never coming back.

Ghosts of Summer

I found you, breaking holes in the ice,
        searching for a perfect snowflake
                in a prison of shattered tears and frozen rain.

            I slid down the winter slope of your smile,
        hypnotized by the frost in your eyes,
warmed by the heat of your body.

        We huddled together
                safe in the depth of our breath,
                        in the catch of our desire;
                a fire running wild in the blood
        stained with the amber residue
                of Nirvana spinning blue.

Hands clasped tightly and skin pressed together,
        on a cold dark night we crept away
                sliding down the curve of winter's back
                        while she lay sleeping.

We travelled light with the ghosts of summer
            into a surreal season
                    of broken rainbows and fading sunsets.
                    We slid down the spine of autumn,
                chased by the shadows of summer,
            as the sun grew dim and burned out
in the freeze of winter's breath.

I left you, breaking holes in the ice,
            searching for the lost ghosts of summer
inside an endless winter.

            I had to leave…
                    I'd stopped believing in ghosts.

Take a Long Look

Take a long sunburnt look
                    at the moonglow
                    spilling out of your heart's unzipped pocket.

            It's calcified and harsh now:
            ice replacing snow;
smooth silk turned to jagged rock;

            and we can't even talk anymore.

Take a long wind-burnt look
                    at the sunset
                    fading into the shadows of your mind.

            It's muted and stunted now:
            grey replacing blue;
twilight turned to darkest night;

            and we don't really see each other anymore.

Take a long look
            at what we didn't see;

                    and ... what we didn't say.

All Great Love Affairs

There is a pulling together
and rending apart
that is basic to, and the essence of,
all great love affairs.

Smiles without tears lose their value
in a bargain basement
of safety nets and guarded hearts.

Swimming close to shore,
with the safety of sand underfoot,
you never feel the bittersweet thrill
of passion's sharp hook sinking into your heart.

Jumping in over your head
into dangerous uncharted waters
you feel the thrill of the current,
the frenzy of rip tides, the angst of the whirlpool
that renders you helpless:
spinning you every way but loose;
burning a hole in your soul;
creating seductive storms and raging tsunamis
where even the harshest slice of love's knife
soothes the willing heart.

Sometimes deep wounds
create beautiful scars:
The trophies of deep emotion.
The residue of all great love affairs.

I still wear you like a medal...
Lest I forget.

Avenue

The avenue ends right here:
where there are no other roads,
where there are no other eyes but his.

           Inside this moving fog,
              chilled with winter's breath,
       he is the dark, shaped mauve at the corners.

           The world spins faster
           as he touches the wind,
           touches my heart.

The first time I saw him,
I felt his heart bleeding through mine.

             The answers were all there.
       Eternity ceased to exist for a moment,
                for all time,
             for almost no time at all.

He is the scar on my sky.
His tears are the depth of my ocean.

      His whispers and voice
      are the only sounds I hear.

            His song is a scythe
            slicing through my being.

     I can't kill him or silence him.

I feel the universe tighten
in the blaze of his eyes.

I hear it cry out
beneath his hypnotic voice.

      The avenue ends right here:
      where there are
            no other roads;
      where there are
            no other eyes.

Too many Suns have died
in my ever-shrinking universe.
         Too many stars have imploded
         in my emotional void.

I can't kill him or silence him.

I step into the night.
        A teardrop builds,
        bursts forth,
    creating new seas of emptiness.

I hold tight to the dark
in frantic desperation.
        Nothing moves,
    but I know there is life around me.
     I can feel it at the core.

                                    I am on the outside.
                            There are no paths leading in.
                        My heart will not beat much longer.

        I can't kill him or silence him.

The avenue ends right here:
where there are no other roads;
where there are no other eyes ...

                            Where he waits.

Coda

In a trilogy of tender torment
three words spilled from a satin shoe
and danced our dreams to death.

I'm leaving you.

This orchestration of punctured sentiment
was out of tune and we were out of time
in the legato of long overdue staccato,
suspended endings.

Sliding down a jagged treble clef
of silent screams
into the bass-ment
of booming reality,
our tangled tablature
weaves itself into a slick loose tempo
that can't be deciphered;
though the words ring out in striking clarity.

I'm leaving you.

In a singularity of certain death
and swift shot rebirth,
the trilogy of tender torment ends,
and a new song emerges!

Coda…

Prayers

I prayed for you.

    You came,
        stayed awhile and then left me alone
            pacing in circles without a compass
                in the middle of a rain forest,
                    heavy with tears.

The world was full of forgetting,
    but I was full of remembering:
        promises broken
            and contracts signed
            with invisible ink;
      deep scars,
            the residue of jagged dreams
            and sleepless nights.

The truth is...
    you are not here;
        and yet, you are always here:
            the raw red heartbeat of night,
                the long, wet tears of day.

    Finding my way out of this rain
        and these tears,
    I covered my tracks
        so I'd never find this forest
            or you again.

Blessed are those prayers
that remain
unanswered.

Wounded Stone Angel

I'm a bittersweet vine,
a wounded stone angel
rooted in cemented feelings;

     a midnight dreamer
     written into a book of strangers
     parading through meaningless chapters;

          a clumsy participant
          chained to the pain of a harsh caress.

I'm insoluble water
locked in a prison of fire and ice;
          a wounded bird
          mired in an oil-slicked ocean.

I don't go around mirrors:
     don't want to see

          the slits of my paper cut eyes,
          the jagged incision of my butchered smile;
     don't want to peer
          through the streaked windows of my heart
          at the scattered carnage of lost love affairs.

I'm a wounded stone angel
dancing to broken records
and rusty compact discs.

Crumbling like ancient cement,
I compact myself into a lopsided smile
      and slowly disintegrate to dust on the wind

     leaving no trace
        of the wounds I sustained ...
           leaving no scars on the stone.

Naked Leavings

Love is like virginity.
When it's gone it's gone;
almost like it never was.
No more sweet nothings
perched upon the lips; wings now clipped.
No lingering traces of tenderness
lurking in the corners of the heart.
Only a foggy dark cemetery
littered with desecrated tombstones.

Lust is like fire.
When it's burnt out it's burnt out;
almost like it never flamed.

No more fever of the soul racing through the mind.
No more aching in the heart to touch the flesh of another.
No more desire to become lost
inside the dreams of the beloved.
Only a cold, neglected fireplace
strewn with yesterday's ashes.

Heartbreak is like a fatal wound.
It always takes you by surprise;
cloaked in deception
hiding under the skin of a lie;
armed with a sharp knife
to make the heart bleed more profusely;
leaving a scar that never truly heals.

Love has many faces;

                some viewed
                through naked leavings.

Sometimes, Dreaming Awake

Sometimes, dreaming awake,
I visualize your face.

Long since lost
at the battered edge of love's broken vows,
I hang in shredded rags:
twisting in a hardened wind,
dangling from a weather-beaten rope,
shorn with blood and tears.

I am the residue of songs
shattered into broken anvils
heavy with flecks of iron tears
that pierce my soul.

Sometimes, dreaming awake,
I see your hazy face.

All my scars are invisible.
All my tears are withered and dry.
All my sorrows abide.

Weeping on a cross of lies,
desecrated by rusty nails.

I am the jagged sunset,
the crumbling mountain,
the dissolving sea,
the broken sky,

You are the broken vow.

Sometimes, dreaming awake,
I imagine you're not gone.

Heart Break

Heart break
            silently:

                        No riotous reverberations.
                        No ear-splitting sounds.

Hearts mend
            soundlessly:

                        No threads puncturing fleshy fabric.
                        No noisy needles knitting.

            Hearts break

                        like waves in a vacuum.

            Hearts mend

                        like bruised atmosphere.

Silence Roars

Silence roars
                          an untamed river
          rushing through the space   between us.

There are gaps   and holes
          in us now:

                          An emptiness we carry
                          in frayed pockets.
                A hollow feeling
                hidden behind love's broken zipper.

There are boundaries   and edges
                    surrounding us now;
                          areas of desolation
                                we dare not risk entering.

          Every day the silence   between us
                          grows, growls

     We have nothing in common,
                    so, we don't talk anymore.

Silence roars
                like an untamed river
                    rushing through
                                    the space
                          between   us.

Intangibles

The tonal quality of voice.
The temperature of body.
The polish and shine in the eyes.

      The grand importance of these
          is sometimes put asunder;
          and I am left to wonder
              at the insufficient attention I paid
          to these seemingly innocuous traits:
          not realizing the voice would become abrasive;
      the temperature. intolerable;
the polish and shine in the eyes would fade.

      Now, standing under the thunder,
          inside a harsh, dull, icy hell
              just beyond the rain,

          I realize
              the extreme importance of intangibles.

Only Fleeting

Your powerful words
       sliced over my shoulder,
              passed by my ears,
                         slingshot style.

The message missed its mark.

Your powerful eyes
       tried to hold me hypnotized;
              but I could not be paralyzed.

      The fire in your gaze burned out,
        fell as dead embers.

      Absorbed in a web of delicate silence
      I continued walking
         through my private paracosm
         oblivious to
             your powerful words
             and fiery gaze.

      Fire burns out.
      Hearts break.
          Love dies;

       and your power
         always was … only fleeting.

Raging Epiphanies

Hail and stone.
Raging epiphanies in opposition.

Call them our hearts.

I see the hard truth in your eyes.
Let sacred words spill from my head
and fall as armour around my soul.

Snow and rock
spin the world to glossy white;
exhale it with a razor's edge
to slice the purple haze
into hail and stone
and brand their scar onto our hearts.

Truth has evaporated.
Words have been silenced.

My armour has turned to rust.
Your heart has crumbled to dust.

Locked in twinned orbits
of bizarre opposition,

we are…

the raging epiphanies.

Veil

Behind the One-Way Mirror

They live.
    They do live on
        in that other hazy dimension
            just beyond our reach.

They walk.
    They still walk
        the shadows of our minds,
            turning memories on and off,
                in cinematic film clips of days past.

They dance
    to their own rhythm;
        feathers brushing
            against our being,
                echoing...
                "Remember me."

They breathe
    their presence into our souls
        to fill the empty space
                they left in us...
                when they left us.

We live.
    We do live on
    behind this one-way mirror
            just beyond their reach,

            waiting ...

        for the mirror to shatter.

The Only Moment

Ekphrastic poem written to painting "Angels (Paradise)" 1909
by M.K.Ciurlionis (1875-1910)

A broken winged lament has brought me to this moment;
    felled me to my soiled knees
        in search of something resembling forgiveness.

    I am alone in a throng of untethered symbionts,
        surrounded by distorted songs
            and discordant memories.
    I cannot lift my head.
        I can only stare at the scattered pebbles,
          disguised as heavenly flowers,
             hoping to be able to grasp
      and decipher their muted whispers and screams,
          searching for the other side of my soul
    I abandoned so very long ago.

I can feel there is a golden tide of dreams

               just beyond my reach.
I can hear a flutter of wings above me

               just beyond my sight;

        and hidden from my knowledge,
      just behind the shapeshifting clouds,
    I know eternity rests
in the technicolour palm
    of the creator's right hand.

With his left hand,
I can feel him lift his brush of many colours,
      breathing life into death
          just beyond this realm.

In my mind I can see him
painting me into paradise,
        just beyond this moment,
          into the only moment
            that ever will matter.

Nights of Your Ghost

There are nights,
    illuminated by scarlet moons,
        bleeding tears into my eyes.
            These are the nights of the dead;
        the nights your ghost
          wanders across the dimly lit skies of my mind,
    against a garish backdrop
of a sequinned indigo curtain.

I fade into the diamond dust
    trying to grasp the threads of your essence
        and press them to my breast.

    Solid...
    then hazy;

        hazy...
        then gone.

Grasping at frayed threads,
    I chase this dream I can't catch.

        I quicken my pace
      as the diamond dust swirls
    in a world of its own illusions,
haunting the sweet of my bones.

      There are nights like this;
      the coveted nights of your ghost.

Ice Age

In my dream
>> I saw you walking toward me
>>> through a field of virgin snow,
>> marking your territory;
>>> new footprints glistening beneath frost-laden branches
>> that reached down to touch you and welcome you home.

>> The next day
> you found me melting stones
>> at the edge of an iceberg,
>>> candling the night,
>>>> burning it down to the core.

>> You held the last of the dying embers
>>> in your icy palm.
>>>> In a strange, yet familiar ceremony
>>> we watched embers burn and ice melt.

In my dream
>> I saw you walking away.

>>>> I closed my eyes
>>> then opened them to look again.

>> Your footprints had dissolved
>>> in a sea of snow.

Death

Death is agony;
a burning-off of the body

        to free the soul.

        The coming apart
        of Siamese twins.

The final breath;
a gasping eventide song
sung with uncertainty.

        Death, our final freedom,
            crossed more frighteningly

        than thin
           crack - ing
                ice.

And I Knew

I saw my mother sitting in my living room;
    where she sat the room was aglow
        emanating all colours of the rainbow.

    She did not see me, watching from the staircase.
        A mirror image,
            tangled in the broken spokes of time,
      slowly she moved from shadow to starlight
        as I stirred to move toward her.
      Dew's cathedral opened to the yawning rose
        she held in her fragile hand, glistening,
    within the ancient reflections of my soul;

Her shadow, stretched out before me,
      began to diminish and fade;
    my own, in established disobedience,
        dissolved into a river she could not swim.
    She turned in slight confusion.
        I heard the uneven beat of her heart.
    The atmosphere thickened.
        Strange mahogany doors rose-up, flew open.

A crystal chandelier stood glittering;
    I saw my mother
        haloed in an amber aura.
        I stepped into the golden embrace of her flame;
    and my mother wept.

Stripped to the bone,
standing immortal in her shroud of tears,
sunlight and ice bound her eyes
into frozen cameras
and sliced her tongue,
so she could not speak of the sins
she had witnessed laying at my feet.

A tear fell.
She dissolved
into the thick of the atmosphere.

The exhaled breath of the night
composed her simple eulogy,

I saw my mother
sitting in my living room
and I knew ...
she wasn't dead.

After I've Gone

I will be gone when you wake tomorrow,
        but I do not leave you empty handed.

    To you, my lover, I leave:

My thoughts to mingle with your daydreams
        that you may resist the reality that I have really gone.
My words to echo in your castigated ears
        that grew conveniently deaf as I spoke of my truths.
My stone-cold silence to your icy lips
        that have so casually bruised my heart.
My second sight to your fragile artistic fingers
        that they may try to paint the love I offered you.
And finally, my four bank accounts with nothing in them
        that you may empty them when you are in need.

    To others:

I leave my misdirected passion to the broken-hearted
        still searching for a Nirvana that cannot be found.
To the ragamuffins and beggars in the street,
        I leave wishes owed to me that I failed to collect.
To my many disposable friends, cut-out doll kings and queens,
        I leave the meaningless ambitions and fleeting fame
            I found lying beside a graffiti-scarred dumpster
                in a blind alley alive with a million lacklustre eyes.

To everyone:

I will be gone when you wake tomorrow.
       but I do not leave empty hearted;

              no, I do not leave empty hearted …

                     I was a poet!

Spirit

A Pleated Movement of Rippled Water

In a pleated movement of rippled water
                I saw God sewing the earth to the sky.

                  And now I search for that first point of puncture;
              that golden needle mark
tattooed on the lip of a drifting horizon.

                  With crows on my shoulders
              and stars in my eyes,
                  I climb into the maze
                      of a sleeping shaman's dream
              where slices of time
                    lay scattered in space.

Laying claim
        to my own predestined slice of time,
                  I ride on the shoulders of crows,
            threading the eye of the needle
        into the pleated movement of rippled water
        where God speaks to me
in the infinite language of crows.

Unsung

I sing the nameless song
with unsung lyrics.

     I walk down a street of long shadows.
        Artifacts of a stone-age sun
           reflect in broken shards
               in the mirrors of my mind.

I take repast
    at a table suspended in air;
       read an invisible menu;
          digest transient nourishment
     in a static ocean
that has no shorelines.

    At rest in the echo of wet deerskin
       I lay in a bed of quantum dreams
      surrounded by slices of time,
         rotating in surreal dimensions
         of yin and yang whispers;
              wet to the touch,
              yet dry as bone.

I sing the nameless song
with unsung lyrics,
    slingshot past sun, moon and stars
       in the tranquil pause between heartbeats.

     In tune with the universe
   I am the nameless song.
I am the unsung lyrics.

Poets' Dance

Hazy circles of possibilities
    vibrate and float haphazardly, touching down
       onto the squares of desperation
          that invade every-day existence.
      We remain unanswered questions
inside this massive silence that holds all the answers.

    All things pass away
    then come to pass again.

Do not wait to step into the sunshine of your soul.
    The best part of you is beckoning you
       to dive into the pristine white waters
         of the poets' surreal dance
      where unfinished songs seeking completion
find their long-lost keys and become seen and heard:
      where liquid, quicksilver lightning
         shakes the foundations of the mind
         and rocks the questing heart
            in the cradle of great expectations.

The wheel of fate keeps spinning toward you,
    waiting for you to claim your dreams.   .
       Follow the path of quills and ink stains
         that penned the broken letters of death
      onto the well-worn parchment of life.

All things pass away
then come to pass again.

We are all searching for the God particle
quite unaware that we are the God Particle.

Look inward angel…
Step into the poets' dance.

Ever-Changing

Inside a pocket of indigo time
       I stood cloaked in white clover
invading the privacy of still waters unstirred for centuries,
        blending coveted pieces of breath
           into shallow pools of blood,
               bringing life to the lungs of the universe,
           opening the lips of eternity
      to form the word; and it was good;
                    and it became poetry;
                    it became healing.

In the ever-changing pool of cosmic consciousness,
       everything is a ripple effect. Everything begins with you.
Hold this thought gently in your mind.
        The waves holding the image are flowing to your shore.
               The tide is yours to turn.

We are the creations, and the creators,
       wrapped in the tumbling yin and yang
        and superconscious illusion,
           ever-changing, becoming reality.

      Healing flourishes in silence.
Stand resolute in your own still, small silence.
       Thrust your hand into your solar plexus
        and grasp your creative force.

In one swift motion pull your hand out
and fling its contents skyward.
The sun, moon, and stars
will appear in sparkling array, ever-changing.

As you will it…
so it will be.

Everything begins with you.

Liquid Flame

A passionate moment in time
                passes through itself,
                                collapses.

A bittersweet taste
whets my lips.
                    Rain falls;
                        shines the day
                        to a fine gloss.

A straw tinder box of abstractions
          kindles itself into glorious flame
                                anointing my feet

          that I may keep pace
                    with a new quickening
          that burns in an orchestration
                    of deafening silences.

Inside the surreal breath
of this invisible rhythm
          I embrace the ringing in my ears
and dance through a magical weave
          of forgotten wishes

                                spinning them real.

          In the wake of distant thunder
          the tinder box turns to ash.

An angel's wing grazes my soul;

                                I turn to liquid flame.

Living Fire

Born from a wayward spark of dust

we are:
>the breath of dreams
>>becoming life;

>fire ablaze
>>in the eternal now;
>>>our waxing and waning heartbeats,
>>>>our rising and falling chests
>>>burning in unison
>>with the cosmic flame.

We are:
>embers spilled
>>from the dust of stars;
>>>sparks bursting into flame;
>>>>brilliantly lighting the days;
>>>warming the edges of night;
>>peeling the black off the dark.

We are;
>spark,
>flame.

>>We are ... living fire.

The Gap Between Pulse and Breath

I dipped my empty pen
     in the blood of a wish;
          scrawled words
          in the air
               and hieroglyphs
               onto the spine of the wind.

Snugging the gap
     between pulse and breath,
          I became star seed and dust
               undulating in binary dance
                    and intricate steps,
             paying lip service
        to the gods
                        through the eye
                        of eternity's flame.

Loosening the gap
     I exited the blood of the wish

               reborn and baptized.

     Comfortable now,
          and pen suffused
               with living ink,

                    I have become the words.

Surreal

Lightning

the night shatters
into eye candy

                                  stabbed and sliced open
                                  by forked lightning

                yellow gold splashed
                on an ebony canvas

the sky

                a glazed wet
                glistening eye
                lighting up

                                  an old Chevy truck,
                                      all rusty
                                  except for glints
                                      of white paint

almost invisible
at the edge of the field

                                  an old scarecrow
                                  that's seen better days
                                  reminds me of myself

                still life
              in the field of life

                                  lightning striking up
                                  old memories

Tuscany

A lemon sun bakes the street's griddle.

Technicolour days fly by like painted doves
    against a backdrop of church bells and laughter.

Inside the smooth pull of a jazz song.
    We languish in this slice of time
    alive with easy living.

The last streaks of sunlight flee through weary streets,
    in the race and chase of approaching night,
    as it rubs its slick black polish
    onto the fading twilight.

A pearl moon waxes the evening horizon.
    Stars sparkle and shimmer
    dusting an ebony tapestry glow
    tossing stardust into our eyes

Sultry nights arrive, parade slowly by
    in a stained-glass cavalcade
    of champagne moments
and strawberry kisses.
We relax in their warm embrace
    and ride on summer winds
    into the breaking dawn.

Time stands still for a moment
　　　before it disappears
　　　　　down eternity's rabbit hole;
　　　　　　but somehow, here,
　　　under the spell of mystic skies,
summer never ends.

White Breath of the Slow-Moving Clouds

From the shallows this side of the deep,
nestled inside a circle of pebbles and sand
a torn swatch of sequined cloth
gleams beneath a broken seashell,
polished to a glittering shine
by the white breath
of the slow-moving overhead clouds;

   and oh how fascinating,
   this evidence of a past event:
      perhaps a lover's moonlight tryst
      beneath a star scattered ebony blanket;
   perhaps an ancient remnant of dress
   torn from a sunken ocean liner's passenger;
perhaps the down from the wing of a wayward angel
flying too close to the ground;
         or perhaps the quantum manifestation
         of an ivory feather coming to rest
         on the pristine silence of imagination.

   Whispers of sugar dusted songs
   drip from the edges of eternity.

If we listen intently,
   we can hear the thunderous sound
      of one hand clapping,
         in a library hushed with words
           too beautiful to be uttered.

Splashes of beauty
spin this scene
a glowing shade of light

as clouds slowly blow the day away.

Angels Sang

Angels sang and circled our souls
           weaving us into the fabric
                of their eternal song.

     We walked on the slick satin water
       of a fast-moving river.

          We ran the rapids.
       flanked by surreal forests and petrified trees.

       Eagles circled above;
           sentinels of our souls.

Inside this surreal forest
      we held hands
          and danced with the past
    as familiar music turned the pages of life,
         writing us into an epic symphony.

Dressed in neon shoes
             and emerald songs
          we waltzed the backlit side
    of a waning moon
         inside the well-worn palm
           of a lesser God.

Human Crush

The lights
are hazy
like dawn
awakening the sea;

                    skulking
                    over it,
                    under it;
                    searching
                    for something lost.

Legs and arms
resurrect dead voices
hidden inside forgotten promises,
broken deeds and unsigned covenants.

Hands and feet
without shape,
nondescript,
become concrete
grasping for something lost.

Here inside this human crush,
the devil in miniature
adds raw red need
to each bite
of forbidden fruit.

Last Train from Avignon

I sit at the edge on the black side of darkness,
        headed toward the final station
              on the last train from Avignon.
Ghosts come out to play with my mind.
        Disembodied voices, tangled in vines and veins
           hanging from broken branches in my heart,
              chant their shrill incantations
            lacerating my soul with rusty spears and arrows
      pillaged from yesterday's battles.

        Inside this speeding metal cocoon,
        travelling toward the final destination,
        I am lashed to the cross of frailty;
        vulnerable to past sordid deeds.

I have seen the scarred underbelly
      of love's most treacherous wars.
        I have seen the blood of lovers
            running rampant over broken hearts,
                victims of their own fragile innocence;
        and more of these atrocities
        will be perpetrated in the name
      of the dark angel, turned ghostly,
sitting beside me tonight.

        The black lips of night whisper my name,
        as this dark angel that knows no mercy
        takes my hand and leads me away
        from everything I've ever known,
        into the black side of darkness.

A Stranger's Paradise Lost

A red, rising sun
        burns and churns
in this mist covered prison
       of stale dreams
                that bind my eyes
                      with ice and fire.

I become a mountain
crying rivers and splinters of dust
            over the slick black rocks
                of a stranger's paradise lost.

            With the sharp stiletto of hope
         I walk through dampened flames.
      Smoky fingers grasp at my hair
and singe the edge of the sun.

I become a singular flame
        flickering on the horizon,
            baking, blistering,
                turning into a hazy charcoal column
            stretching skyward.

       I burn in slow motion fade out
         like a dying ember
                in a crumbling wet tin.

Beneath a fading red sunset
I scatter in splinters of starlight,
raining in a river of tears,
sliding over a stranger's paradise lost,
trying to carve my way back
into my own.

Dreamer of Dreams

The moon awakens,
        rises in the paling flare of a sultry day.
           The sun disappears
    fleeing from marauding moonbeams;
and stars emerge through ebony windows in the sky.

           A ghostly figure dances on the horizon.

The dreamer of dreams is weaving a dream
        as gorgeous twilight wanders in
        cloaked in lilac and indigo scarves,
           stacked foot upon thigh upon arm upon chest.

I follow this pied piper, this dreamer
        through a thickening mist of purple,
        into the palace of sparkling stars.

        As the wind whirls
        and speaks in a softer voice
        I become aware of many distant voices
        inside the citadel of night.

Above the low hum, I hear him calling.
        His voice, like the breeze, is soft haunting music.
    He dances, as a ghost,
inside a forgotten, familiar song.

The sky is a dazzle of organic starlight:
    flowing, rising, ascending.
  A pressure closes in.
 I feel his warm breath on my neck
    and turn to behold his beautiful face.

The eternal dreamer of dreams
  moves through me
    like finely distilled evening air.
An aching deep
  claws its way to the surface,
    turns to rain, spills over my sleeping spirit,
     falling in keys and tones onto my hollowed-out bones,
     humming familiar songs.

I walk with the dreamer
  along night's crease
    into the hidden secrets of twilight.

Before I entered the dreamscape
  I was an empty song
    collapsed inside empty hours;
     heart charred and raw
      and soaked to the bone
       with the rain I burnt to ash.

So I shook the chill off night's hard edge
  and my empty song turned to dust,
       fell like snow.

I polished the sky to marble,
and created new songs for the rain to sing;

The dreamer of dreams
heard them ringing
and wove another beautiful dream.

Alive in the Paint

From shadow to light, purple to white,
      nestled in colours of death and life,
            I pick up my brush in the soft candle-glow
     to paint an emotion i know will flow
          with passion, lust, love and romance,
               fabulous rhythm and eloquent dance,
        where the blessed, the frail and obscurely quaint
              are part of the brilliance, alive in the paint.

Then I take a step back and step out of the picture
to analyze the paint and survey the mixture.

I put down my brush and cross the floor
     and gaze into the mirror that hangs on the door.
        I stare at my image in shock and surprise
    at the secrets hiding behind my eyes.
        I see evidence of old truths tossed away
           where guilty pleasures held court and held sway
        dipping my world into indigo ink.
           clouding my judgement 'til I couldn't think;
        couldn't differentiate right from wrong;
          a symphony from a rock'n'roll song.

So I polished my breath until it came to rest
on the satin lapel of an artist's vest.

Stars sparkled and shone as the darkness undressed.
I fell to my knees and humbly confessed.
The world began spinning a bright shade of white
as I moved from the shadow into the light,
delighting the eye in the sky I suppose
because it applauded in quiet repose.
Now, if I listen closely, I can still hear the sound
of that one hand clapping; the other one bound;
then the sound slowly fades and becomes very faint
but something still breathes … alive in the paint.

Acknowledgements

As always, I thank my mentor, the late Fred Cogswell, Member of the Order of Canada and founder of Fiddlehead Poetry Books (now Goose Lane Editions), for his encouragement and his belief in my poetry in the early days so many years ago, when he published my first book, *A Split in the Water* (1979).

I also thank all the publishers, poets, and persons who have crossed my path on my poetic journey. You have all contributed to the person I have become and I thank you all.

I acknowledge the previous publication of the following poems: "Human Crush" (*Wordplay at Work* ezine, 2018); "Lost Edge" (*Royal City Poets Anthology,* 2015); "And I Knew" (*Royal City Poets Anthology,* 2015); "Ghost of Summer" (*Royal City Poets Anthology,* 2014); and "Hearts Break" (*Fiddlehead Poetry Book,s* 1979).

Photo: Ken Ader

Candice James served two three-year terms as Poet Laureate of New Westminster, British Columbia, and was appointed Poet Laureate Emerita by City Council, November 2016. She is author of fifteen books most recently: *Rithimus Aeternam* (2019). Her poetry has appeared in many international anthologies and magazines and her poems have been translated into Arabic, Italian, Bengali, and Farsi. She is Founder of Royal City Literary Arts Society and Founder of the Fred Cogswell Award for Excellence in Poetry and the recipient of the Bernie Legge Artist Cultural Award, and Pandora's Collective Citizenship Award. Candice is also a visual artist, musician, singer/songwriter, workshop facilitator. She lives in New Westminster, BC. For further information, see: https://en.wikipedia.org/wiki/Candice_James and www.candicejames.com.